What to deflect when
you're deflecting

What to deflect when you're deflecting

Jason Morphew

POETS WEAR PRADA • Hoboken, New Jersey

What to deflect when you're deflecting

Poets Wear Prada
533 Bloomfield Street, Second Floor
Hoboken, New Jersey 07030
http://pwpbooks.blogspot.com

First North American Publication 2017
First Mass Market Paperback Edition 2017

Grateful acknowledgment is made to the following publications where some of these poems originally appeared or are forthcoming:

Anamesa, Bellevue Literary Review, The Cortland Review, Santa Fe Literary Review, Soul-Lit, Third Wednesday, and *Venus Magazine.*

ISBN-13: 978-0-9979811-8-6   ISBN-10: 0-9979811-8-0

Printed in the U.S.A.

Front Cover Artwork and Design: Roxanne Hoffman
Author Photo: Morphew Family Archives

For Tilly and Teddy — Love is here.

Table of Contents

What to deflect when
you're deflecting

Pesticide

Dawn swimming deserves
a film of poison
peach fuzz on a kidney
made of glass.
Naked as motivation
viscera willfully neglected
party guests gone
down County Road 89
young woman leaving
satin robe
slipping as archaeologist
into wreckage of my love
cramming me with skeletons
of future ultrasounds
her backward fingers
spelling *if God is dead*
so is the pilot
holding the hatch open
with his frozen mind.

At dawn completely

in my arms
she doesn't know
of dusk
but I do
and what lies
between
is all there is
of us.

Innocence/Perversity

The right way is the wrong way

                              my daughter age 1

dead boy

you wouldn't know it
        to look at him
racquet swinging kitchen dancing baby
        lifting not alive
pulse faked by metronome
        love faked by time
every smile a figment
        of an anonymous
        mind

marriage

babies cry in the womb —
practicing
doctors say.
I think of you and me
(voluntary twins)
passing in the hall
children weeping
in our arms —
aren't they still practicing?
are we?

Evangelical Christianity

No horror is horror
until it is

escaped

carried with you
into your child's face

cross spinning in the DNA
cross rising in the pool
murder moving

through the heart of love.

Acute and Chronic

after Fallen *by Lauren Kate*

My daughter explodes
when told it's time for dinner
her childhood interrupted
by mundane survival.
Did kids explode
before childhood was invented
when no one expected
to do anything but survive
and there was no need
to relinquish plastic duck
molded into medical doctor
holding tiny reflex hammer
wearing white coat and head mirror?
Maybe that quack was about to save her life
who am I to disrupt any diagnosis
it's out of my testicles
now her ferocious life
all I do is usher her into and out of
a little cloud of smoke
trying not to rupture its delicate ringlets
knowing one day I'll return to it
alone.

Does James Brown have a penis?

she asks from her pink toilet
holding in one hand a plastic idol
of the singer and in the other its
corresponding microphone.
Well   hard to describe genitalia of the dead
men have penises.   She gazes at Godfather
of Soul toward the eternal
I take it from her trying to see:
paleblue moundrise paleblue crotch
nothing settled everything obscure
I give the legend back
and mysteriously announce
Men and boys have penises.   Increased nuance
same result daughter's eyes daring doll
to swerve as in videos
just ended. As she stands I want to say
The soul's outside the body
the soul's outside the world
after your bath when you're exhausted
and I drape you in a towel
I am an attending flame
but you are the blaze already
roaring past my arms
my hands my name.

field song

seed of death within me
floating over hidden notches
seed of death within me
where no doctor watches
seed of death within me
does not require water
seed of death within me
cares not about my daughter
seed of death within me
subjectively a dancer
seed of death within me
objectively a cancer
seed of death within me
fleck of shadowed mountain
seed of death within me
drop from blackened fountain
seed of death within me
my blood is flowing soil

reading in darkness

climbing a falling ladder

       drunking a fuck model

praying for silence

       adulterating a child

sipping blood from

       dead ideas

rusting twilight

       sky

Anchor Baby

Two ghosts in purgatory
made an anchor baby.
Because they'd been to grad school
the ghosts loved liminality
and had made a religion of it
which is to say they were afraid
equally of heaven and of hell.
There was something about grad school
those ghosts it attracted
made this religion logical —
fear of failure fear of success
fear of No fear of Yes
fear of Life fear of Death.
What fool wouldn't want to stay
between forever what fool
thinks he takes a side
he can see?

Hence the baby.

No one could say if making life
in such a world was good or evil.
This was the kind of ambiguity
kept the couple getting out of bed
in the afternoon which half
explains the baby's doorway
conception fucking ghosts just un
naked *Weekend at Bernie's* motorboat
audible beyond ancient midterms
slightly read partly stained
wholly graded.

The birth like death
was touch

and go.
Dad worried Mom
wouldn't be
liminal for long.
She survived delivery
to face a shock:

The baby was not a ghost
the baby was real.

Could a living thing remain in purgatory?
It was a contradiction of terms.
As purgatorians texted
the baby unfastened its frenulum
and mixed its mortality with
eternity. This amused
or terrified purgatorians according to depth
of phantom brainhole.
No ghost's superstition mattered
the baby was fine the baby was
reasonable. Some aspects of purgatory it enjoyed —
stark expanses arbitrary fires —
some it didn't (kisses made you colorblind).
The parents were grateful
to the baby for letting them stay
lost ever more thoroughly confused.

After some decades
the baby disappeared
and the parents passed into hell
which after a while they had to admit
through gnashing gums
was preferable to wondering
what might have been
if they were real.

Halogen

Three years ago we came
to the house of twelve million track lights
which live slickly two years
as if powered by hamster
earning master's degree.
Lately climbing the ladder
at six AM to replace another individual
aspect of the whole
as my son slowly pours milk onto the dining table
and my daughter shrieks *I don't like this song!*
groping through the growing abrogation
I wonder if this light will outlive me
this prosthetic of my mind
symbol of my striving
crafted far away by someone else.

Forgiveness

Being neither god nor government
offspring's authority
not of right and wrong
but of left and right
having listened closely
to preachers' warnings
about judging others
having been forgiven
by those I have not wronged
having been wronged
by the same forgivers
as they declared through triumphant tears
my forgiveness is not required
for they have forgiven themselves
(for the wrong wrongs)
actually believing
everyone is equal
I am no forgiver
more of a prayer
for a heaven
where forgiveness is escaped.

Baby in a Blender

The day after she miscarried
again we stumbled into Macy's
our matrimonial blender
was dead we identified
then clutched the most
expensive one they had
a Vitamix brought it home
and blended everything in sight
beets rhubarbs raspberries wine
music mortgage manuscript
our nanny watching with a frightened look
as if remembering the playground
jokes about the quality of red
spinning
everything mixed with everything else
all those vitamins
nourishing the earth
pulling it out putting it inside
love is hilarious
and immature
my lips covered with blood.

Cast of Thousands

You watch your child emerge
from your wife's body then
you take them home and wait
for the idiots to arrive
teachers parents coaches
kids bequeathing borrowed pain
then one night rising
to your retching child you read
in her toy mirror words you forgot
you tattooed on your face:
To know life and its attendant horror
I seek contact with your race.

Let's take it apart

and see what happens
my twoyearold son says
kneeling naked at a Casio
keyboard speaker plugged
into an iPhone resting
on a rock up the slope
of our Laurel Canyon
backyard. My God is
he an engineer? Please
let him be an engineer
save him from the curse
of creativity of whoring
out the heart and mind
on spec to gormless johns
who neither understand nor
pay. Save him from poetry
and music deliver him from
dreams of hammocked spray
into mahogany and money
made of leather flowers
cascading down the opened robes
of the young and sideways
slick. Get him laid God
not too often despite
his shocking dick.
Dare I think it?
Make him happy
as he is here loving
loved and nude.
Dad you're Bacchus
and I'm God he says
ripping the cord out of the speaker
as I take another drink of wine
absolutely screwed.

Summer Transfer Information Banquet

chemical transfers stain
countertop to drawer
lie transfers truth
authenticity to art
wine transfers ecstasy
anxiety to death
sex transfers face
man to child

no journey possible
without destination
no joy possible
without obscurity
no joining
possible
we hope you will apply

Listening to California

For Jason White

don't get out
of my head much —
babies books TV
at night glass in hand
murdering the dream —
sometimes in darkness
I think of friends
it was impossible to keep
we were too starving
alongside each other's
ruthless bodies
scavenging sent us
to eyelined carcasses
in adjacent fields.

Some nights rolling over
I hear a coyote cry
in hunger and I pause
from the private feast
of my secret life.
I peer into the canyon.

Perhaps it's a friend
come from another field
to sing out to me
I love you.

Then I feel the emptiness
from such assumptions
in the past
and I resume my feasting
free to be as faceless
as any passing scream.

family life

tonight the stars have come inside
to satirize sadness
throwing naked shadows
on the little rooms
where we hang our skin
tonight our lawsuits dance
without us
to the rhythm of our children's
lengthening bones
and we are immortal
listening to records

Pike County

One star shines at dusk
above our hot tub in the hills
I can show that to my daughter
in hopes it will encourage the poetic
all children inherit and most
eventually decline.
I have disappeared
and thus notice little.
I'm like a country singer
songwriter suddenly rich
with nothing to write about
and decades not to do it.
Funny thing is I am
a failed country singer
songwriter well I didn't fail
the singing and writing as much
as the cocksucking.
Who can love a spitter?
He doesn't want the pain inside.
Hunger is the only genre.
George and Dolly
learn starving singers' songs
while stretching in gyms to seem
hungry for fat patrons.
George's trainer is now
Guillermo Worm
who escaped dissection
in my wife's Biology
by switching himself
with a gummy.
Corn Syrup is the name
Corpsey George has given him
pronouncing it *Kuhn Srp*.

Guillermo has been around the block
Guillermo is no spring chicken
Guillermo wears a tracksuit
when he eats away your eyes.
There was a worm on my brother's rainy grave
the other day in Glenwood
where everyone believes everything
on *TMZ* with reason.
I believe everything
I am done doubting
the blackness
of my father's lungs
the loving racist things it's done
to his lost and racing heart
failing in Little Rock
succeeding there too
while I see now more stars
appear above my sleeping daughter.

Praying Again

(to Jesus)
and his precious holy name—
what can whispers do
for my children's little hands?
What might a derivative god
stretching walls
of repressed southern hearts
of the 1980s
mean to my babies' bodies
in the next room
now?
Protect them
please God
you're all I know.

Milo

Mounting the museum toilet
she asks when she'll be a boy.
I ask when I'll be a girl.
When you go inside Milo
when you come out you'll be a girl.
She swings her legs and looks above me.
Daddygirl. Mommyboy. Brothergirl. Sisterboy.
So the beast in the family
brindle boxer ancient
as her parents' marriage
is finally recognized
as a portal between sexes
modes of being, physical states
of love
and I am blind
drying hands in the abyss
grasping for her mind
to guide me.

barotrauma

perforating
from heaven
godnailed
in middle ear

What are you looking for Daddy?

lightlessness
obscured by garbage
where my howling
downward
sends you higher
into joy

The Poet Ascends

Having walked the earth and found it
unwalkable I leave you now to prepare
my doorway squat in paradise
which if you've read the Bible closely
has class divisions eviler than earth's
because they're based on prior morality
whose goal apparently was always really
a bigger house. Oh yes it will be hell
in heaven but family and other enemies
will be there so at least you have an
awkward fog of harpies to constantly avoid
which passes the endless time and even
eventually gives you a kind of sense of purpose.
We are who we are because of what we're not
which for me here is living. I was raised wrong
a hilarious thing to say hovering
above the ground looking down women's
blouses. Dad taught me that talent and perseverance
are what matters Mom that Christlike suffering
is what counts. Did you hear *Be professional* or
Kiss fool ass? I didn't think so! Yes my parents
are idiots that's what I love about them it has me
here regretting what I said about blouses
yet crazy enough to fly away from all of you.
Don't tell my children anything. Only this part
of me is leaving. Another part even now does
the hokey pokey making believe he's a robot
playing make believe because even caregivers
need an imaginative entry into games they're not
really supposed to be playing. I know how that sounds
and don't give a fuck having met other parents.
That's what it's all about:
after being trained to impress only God

and future evaluators of ability who like God
may or may not exist when I saw that
my superiors were stupid I was still
in the South with no options of perspective.
Of course I stopped performing
for everyone which is what the earth calls crazy
when the crazy man in question isn't dribbling
on his shirt which I would gladly do if I thought
it would annoy someone I dislike.
Yes I'm leaving you dopes worried
about getting into preschool and whether you
can keep your house. I intend to be homeless
in heaven sleeping in the doorways of mansions
inhabited by the previously morally superior —
no need to be good now! Ensconced baby! What's that?
Am I worried about leaving the atmosphere? Oh no dumbass
and thank you for your support. This asshole logic
I'm only too delighted to escape.
Clearly I'm flying off on faith.
The only ones among you with faith
are the desperately sad because you live
in constant shock at how horrible life here is.
Happy people are groovy with horror
having adjusted their hearts to keep time.
So if I must explain the obvious to dumbfucks
when I reach space I will collapse
into a single unfeeling atom
traveling at medium speed to Wonderland. Capiche?
Once there I will slightly less sadly expand
into the tennised torso you see above you now
knowing he's gone on too long. I hadn't expected
to give a toast but my wife's wailing
sirenized the fire department so I wafted
to witness I'm not beating or raping but

zooming to freedom and transient eternity.
Fuck you all motherfuckers.

[*Entangled in power lines and electrocuted.*]

Is Daddy Dancing?

what my daughter asks
as I turn away
to wash the dishes
as if everything is
part of the party
and all movement
made by a beloved
love

Acknowledgments

The author would like to thank the publishers and editors of the various publications where these poems previously appeared or are forthcoming, sometimes in a slightly different format or version:

"marriage" "family life"	*Anamesa*
"field song"	*Bellevue Literary Review*
"Evangelical Christianity"	*The Cortland Review*
"Listening to California"	*Santa Fe Literary Review*
"Does James Brown have a penis?" "Forgiveness" "Anchor Baby"	*Soul-Lit*
"Halogen"	*Third Wednesday*
"Baby in a Blender"	*Venus Magazine*

About the Author

Jason Morphew started life in a mobile home in Pike County, Arkansas. He holds a PhD in English Renaissance Literature from UCLA. His poems have appeared in *Gigantic*, *Foothill*, *Anamesa*, *Juxtaprose*, *Storm Cellar*, *Third Wednesday*, and *Blue Fifth Review*. A poetry chapbook titled *In Order to Commit Suicide* was published by Floating Wolf Quarterly in 2012. His first full-length volume of poems, *dead boy*, is forthcoming from Spuyten Duyvil. As a singer/songwriter he has released six albums, most recently *Vaporizer* on Max Recordings in 2008, others on the labels Brassland, Ba Da Bing!, and Unread. He lives with his wife and children in Laurel Canyon, Los Angeles, California and teaches English at UCLA.

A NOTE ON THE TYPE

This book is set in Minion Pro, an Old-Style serif typeface designed by Robert Slimbach of Adobe Systems, and released in 1990 by Linotype. Inspired by the mass-produced publications of the late Renaissance, but with a contemporary crispness and clarity not possible with the print machinery of that era, even by the best of the Renaissance typographers, this modern-day interpretation is well regarded for its classic baroque-rooted styling and its enhanced legibility. One of the five or six most widely used typefaces for trade paperback fiction published in the United States over the past several years, Minion Pro is the typeface adopted by the Smithsonian for its logo. The name Minion is derived from the traditional classification and nomenclature of typeface sizes; *minion,* the size between *brevier* and *nonpareil,* approximates a modern 7-point lettering size.